Bygone BURTON UPON TRENT

ON POSTCARDS AND PHOTOGRAPHS

BURTON UPON TRENT

ON POSTCARDS AND PHOTOGRAPHS

TERRY GARNER

First published in Great Britain in 2008 by
The Breedon Books Publishing Company Limited
Breedon House, 3 The Parker Centre, Derby, DE21 4SZ.

This paperback edition published in Great Britain in 2014 by DB Publishing, an imprint of JMD Media Ltd

Thanks to my wife Jean for her patience while compiling my collection, to Mrs Rita Page for help in the initial scanning, Mrs Glynys Cooper at Waterstones for suggesting the book and finally all the anonymous people who over the years have kept these records of Burton's past in collections, shoe boxes, drawers or cupboards to be enjoyed today.

All items in this book are from my own personal collection.

ISBN 978-1-78091-421-3

Printed and bound in the UK by Copytech (UK) Ltd Peterborough

Contents

High Street, Burton-on-Trent.

A very early scene clearly showing the intricate rails of the Corporation tramway line system, with the sweep of the lines turning into Station Street. Briggs shoe shop, seen on the right-hand side, featured on many postcards over the years and finally closed in 2008.

Judging by the amount of people shown here, it must be either a Thursday or Saturday market day in the 1950s. The properties seen on the left are Boots Cash Chemists, Baileys Confectioners and Hiltons Shoe Shop. The Andressey Passage, just along from the shops, will be remembered by many as the way to the YMCA and Memorial Gardens. One of the many thoroughfares in Burton, this is probably the oldest.

High Street from Station Street, BURTON-ON-TRENT (717)

Here is another 1950s view showing the Electric Theatre, which had by then been renamed the Gaumont. This closed in 1959. Opposite was the Marks & Spencer store with its two entrances, this one in High Street and the other round the corner in Station Street. Many people used to use this as a shortcut, especially when it was raining.

Looking back towards Bargates, the public house that is advertising ales and stouts was the Market Hotel, which stood at No.158 High Street and belonged to Cox and Malins Ltd, Wine & Spirit Merchants. There is now a solicitors' office on this site.

This view can be dated to the 1930s because of the title of the film being shown at the Electric Theatre, the western *Nevada*, which was released in 1935. The ornate frontage has now all gone, but the date rosette above the archway entrance can still be seen, as can the small arched doorways on either side.

This is a 1920s view, with the two ladies on the left passing the Black Cat Billiard Hall, which was directly opposite the Electric Theatre. The Wheatsheaf Hotel can be seen to the right of the tradesman's cart.

This view is looking back towards Station Street from the entrance to the Market Place, with Ellis's clothes shop and Povey's Dining Rooms on opposite corners. Everyone in view has stopped going about their business in order to appear on the photograph. No tramlines have been laid as yet, so this picture dates from before 1902.

In 1908 Ellis Men & Boys' Clothing rebuilt the old ground-floor building pictured above to the elaborate one shown below.

This is another pre-1902 view, showing Oakdens, with its famous smell of roasted coffee beans, where the two girls are standing on the left. The horse and cart are standing outside the White Hart Hotel, which was the place where the hiring of manual servants took place at the time of the Statutes Fair. Deliveries to local villages by various carriers departed from here.

Moving forward approximately 70 years, and all the shops, with the exception of Birds, have changed business. Shortly after this postcard had been issued it was decided to pedestrianise High Street.

Abbey Drapery occupied the corner plot of the Abbey Arcade for many years, and after it closed the property was split into smaller units. A branch of the local company Roberts & Birches Butchers stood next door, which is now H.J. Richards Jewellers.

At the north end of High Street next to the Bargates Centre was Eatoughs Shoe Factory, which employed many local people. The large buildings next to it were part of the Bass Old Brewery. Both of these structures are no longer standing.

Here is a row of Bass cottages numbered 70–73 Station Street, all of which were demolished along with Drapers Florist and Greengrocers in 1983. There is now no sign of what stood here before.

Following the removal of all these properties, Drapers being the last occupied, the area was landscaped and the Bass Barrel fountain is situated here.

Station Street, Burton-on-Trent.

An image of the Station Street junction with Guild Street and Union Street, dating from when the gas and electric showrooms occupied the shops on the right. The policeman standing on the corner seems to be having a very quiet day. The property with the hoardings on the side was occupied by Derbyshire Farmers.

This photograph has been taken from further down the street and none of these shops now survive, the properties having changed to a variety of building societies, charity shops and fast food outlets. The car parked on the right-hand side is outside what is now the pedestrian entrance to Burton Place.

STATION STREET, BURTON-ON-TRENT.

H.7343.

Station Street, Burton-on-Trent.

Here, a hansom cab is making its way down the Station Bridge, probably carrying passengers who have just arrived by train, passing the block known as Midland Chambers. Apart from the shops changing business, little else has altered at this end of the street.

This photograph shows the junction from another angle, with two Burton Corporation trams in view. It gives the impression that the Roebuck Inn on the right has disappeared, but it survives to this day. The cottages on the left were not so fortunate, having been demolished some years ago.

This photograph of the High Street and Station Street junction shows a clear view of the Wheatsheaf Hotel in the foreground on the right. Touring artists appearing in the town would sometimes stay here. The uniformed man in the middle of the road is probably a tramways employee. The paperboy seems to have decided this was a good opportunity to have his photograph taken.

This is a picture of the same view in either the late 1950s or early 1960s. The Wheatsheaf had been replaced by John Collier Tailoring, although this has also now disappeared. The Barclays Bank on the left has now moved further up High Street, and the site has been occupied by the Philadelphia Stores and later the Grand Clothing Hall.

A Burton Corporation tram heading into town en route to the Branston Road terminus, with passengers alighting outside the Midland Hotel (now the Grail Court). This was the nearest stop in town for Horninglow residents visiting the Opera House in Guild Street.

Moving forward approximately 30 years, the overhead tram stanchions have now been converted to carry street lights and the tram stops are now used by the Corporation buses. The Opera House had become the Ritz Cinema by this time.

Tucks postcard publishers covered the country with their famous 'oilette' series of cards. Burton was no exception, with six cards being issued – this one being their interpretation of Station Street.

This is a very quiet scene looking from George Street corner. None of the shops seen in the photograph have survived, the properties on the right having been demolished to make way for the large Sainsbury's store that stands there today. The Wesleyan Church was demolished in the late 1950s, having stood on this corner since 1871.

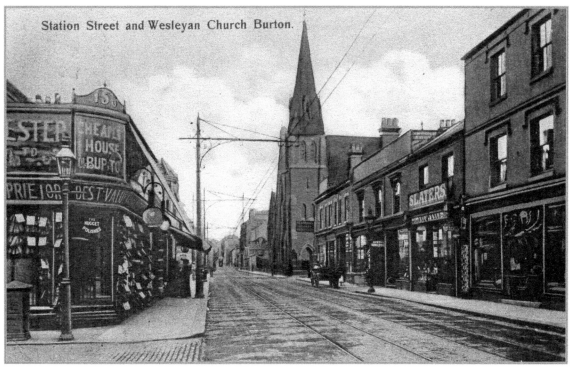

This photograph shows the line of houses between the Coopers Tavern (then still a Bass house) and the welfare clinic at the far end of Cross Street, which were cleared for regeneration at the same time as those on Milton Street.

The Milton Street terraced houses leading towards Duke Street awaiting demolition in the 1980s, which were all later replaced by modern dwellings.

A very early view from the top of St Paul's Church looking towards the town, with the cottages of St Paul's Street East still in existance, facing the town hall. Opposite the town hall clock tower, the pub sign that belonged to the Dolphin Inn can just be seen.

This photograph shows the Grange Street corner with St Paul's Street West, with the main entrance doorway to St Paul's Church visible in the distance.

A Burton and Ashby tram travelling towards the police station en route to Ashby along a deserted Guild Street.

The shop and cottages on Guild Street awaiting demolition in the 1980s, numbered from 66 to 79. There was also a line of cottages behind these that were numbered 66A to 69A which were accessed via the passage by the wall in the right-hand corner.

These large properties on Guild Street were where Frankie & Benny's restaurant now stands. The house on the left was number 63, and the one on the right was number 64, and this, along with number 65, was served by the central arched entrance just visible over the hedge.

Cottages, shops and the flour mill of J. Lever & Co (the white building) in Horninglow Street, all of which were demolished in the 1980s. The large property of Geo. Hodges offices is the only one still there today.

The row of cottages and the Friends meeting house have all long since gone from this section of Abbey Street, from Lichfield Street to the windows of the Leopard Inn on the right. The property at the far end was at one time the Marquis of Anglesey public house.

Standing between Hawkins Lane and the police station, these Ind Coope fire service cottages are all boarded up waiting for demolition, photographed in the 1980s. The large building in the centre to the left of the gateway with the white upper bay window was the gatehouse and weighbridge exit.

Uxbridge Street in the early 1900s, looking towards Moor Street. In earlier times the stretch between Park Street and Moor Street was known as Church Street, before it was eventually incorporated into Uxbridge Street.

This building here, on the George Street–Station Street corner, at this time owned by A.J. Rutter, was one of the last surviving independent bakeries in Burton, lasting well into the 1970s as Manlove's.

The Electricity Board offices stood next to the crossing gates and Holy Trinity Church in Horninglow Street until they were demolished in the late 1960s.

The junction of Horninglow Street and Guild Street photographed in the 1980s. The only building still standing is the large one on the corner behind the lamp-standard. Goodhead's butchers, Turner's fish & chip shop, Gough's taxis and the cycle repair shop are all gone.

A much quieter scene at the Belvedere Road junction with what is Calais Road today. Most of the traffic using this route now do so to access the Burton and District Hospital Centre.

Branston Road looking towards town, with the Corporation tram lines clearly visible. All Saints Road junction is to the left and the wall of All Saints' Church can be seen on the right.

This large building on Duke Street and Mosley Street corner has had many uses in its time, starting out as the Burton Charity Organisation Society, then Burton Scouts' Room, Robirch Sports and Social Club and finally as a base for training apprentices for the building trade.

This photograph shows the last surviving soup kitchen building in Burton just before its demolition. The words 'Soup Kitchen' can just be made out despite the fact that they had been filled in. The property survived for just over 100 years, having been built in 1880.

A postcard view looking from the Station Bridge showing how grand the Victorian buildings were. These all disappeared in 1971 and were replaced by the buildings that are there today.

This photograph shows the marvellous frontage that was removed during modernisation. Many people will remember that there always seemed to be a smell of fresh fish as you entered the booking hall, which was just behind the horse and cart on the right.

44,10 The Railway Station, Burton-on-Trent

The Derby–Birmingham side of the station, photographed in the early 1900s. The kiosk of WH Smith provided newspapers, books, postcards and confectionery for many years.

The *Tutbury Jinnie* awaiting the signal to move off. After making its run on 11 June 1960 the line closed.

The Church Lads' Brigade from Winshill are about to board a train to take them to their annual camp. The brigade were formed in 1900.

Falling in for an inspection, probably by Colonel Goer who started the CLB for lads aged between 13 and 19. Attendance was required on two nights a week, one for drill and one for Bible class.

Although the caption on this postcard states that the bridge is under construction, it does in fact show the bridge widening that took place in 1924–26.

This earlier postcard clearly shows how narrow the bridge had been in the early part of the 1900s. It was not altered for over 20 years.

TRENT BRIDGE, BURTON-ON-TRENT.

An unusual view of the bridge from the bank, with the River Trent in very low flow.

Most postcard views like this one of the Trent Bridge were taken from the swimming baths side, and this one shows the roadway down to Meadow Lane.

Trent Bridge. Burton-on-Trent.

COPYRIGHT.
B.T. 39.

TRENT BRIDGE IMPROVEMENT. BURTON-ON-TRENT.

LILYWHITE LTD.,
TRIANGLE. HALIFAX.

The widening of the Swan junction had obviously been deemed a success as it was thought appropriate to issue a postcard showing the improvement.

Another postcard showing the bridge, but it is still very quiet. The shelter, telephone kiosk and shrubs have been added to the island.

Trent Bridge, Burton-on-Trent.

A 1920s postcard view from Bridge Street showing little traffic. The exit from the left is still only a narrow roadway.

A view into the town giving a clear picture of the complex overhead tram cables and the wide variety of traffic using the bridge, which includes a Corporation tram, a lorry, cars, bicycles, horse carts and handcarts.

A large crowd of onlookers for the Ladies' Walking Match, part of the 1917 Patriotic Fair. There were two matches, as they were called, one for single and one for married ladies, both of which started on Stapenhill Hollow.

The 6th North Staffordshire Infantry Brigade making their way accross the bridge toward Winshill in preparation for mobilisation. They were one of the first units to be sent to France in World War One.

A clear view of the idyllic setting for this inspiring property by the banks of the River Trent at the Winshill end of the bridge.

In the 1920s, after the bridge had been widened, mud boards and iron railings were added. They were all later removed and the railings were melted down for use during World War Two.

Looking down from Bearwood Road with a clear view of the straight run taken by the trams off and on to the bridge.

Postcards of the time show how open the Swan junction was. The errand boy has stopped to watch the photographer and the road sweepers seem to be ambling across the road, neither concerned about any traffic.

Leaving the bus park could sometimes be a very tight operation, as can be seen in this photograph, and cars being allowed to park nearby only complicated matters.

This Corporation bus on 'Special' service is leaving to go into town. Behind it, it can be seen how steep the slope down into the bus park was. The workman at the bus stop is waiting for either the number 1 or number 2 bus to Stapenhill.

Wetmore Road Bus Station at the town end of the Trent Bridge had defined bays for the various bus companies. Here the Trent bus on the Hatton route stands beside a double decker of Stevensons, just visible.

Photographed below is the exit gateway on to the bridge, with the Midland Red number 704 service to Ashby about to leave. The wooden waiting rooms and the cafeteria building are on the right.

A high flood, as seen from the Stapenhill side. The swimming baths, Holy Trinity Church, brewery chimneys and the pumping station, later the dog pound, have all vanished from this view.

No collection of views of the Trent Bridge would be complete without one looking down to the sheds of Burton Rowing Club and the Leander Rowing Club. Most people walking over the bridge would instinctively look down at this scene.

A scene posed for the photographer, taken before Corporation tramcar number 16 began its journey from outside St John's Church to Branston Road.

Horninglow Church, Burton-on-Trent.

A slightly unusual postcard view looking from Dover Road corner. The hoarding was informing people that the Opera House was closed.

The Royal Oak public house on the left still survives to this day, minus the trees by the roadside. The right-hand side of the road has totally changed.

Horninglow station platform, together with the signal box on Derby Road, photographed in the 1960s. The station building survived as a café for many years after the line closed.

HORNINGLOW NIGGER MINSTRELS 1909.

This local entertainment troupe had a title that would no longer be allowed today.

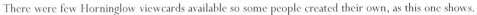

There were few Horninglow viewcards available so some people created their own, as this one shows.

LOVE FROM HORNINGLOW

Volunteers return from S. Africa. Old In the market place. Parish Church Buxton

Every vantage point on the shops and church was taken by the crowds to watch the volunteers of the South African conflicts of the early 1900s return to attend a commemorative service with local dignitaries, which was held for them at the Parish Church.

A proclamation by the Lord Mayor in front of the Parish Church. It is believed to be the announcement of the new king, George V, on 6 May 1910, due to the size of the crowd. The public house is the Royal Oak.

Parish Church and Market Square, Burton-on-Trent.

Deserted except for two carts, this postcard shows the market place on a wet morning in the 1940s.

A very busy market place with 'Chippy Heaps' stall, with the white canopy, in the foreground and to its left 'Rondes' ice cream stall. In the distance, standing directly in front of the Parish Church, there appears to be a showman's attraction.

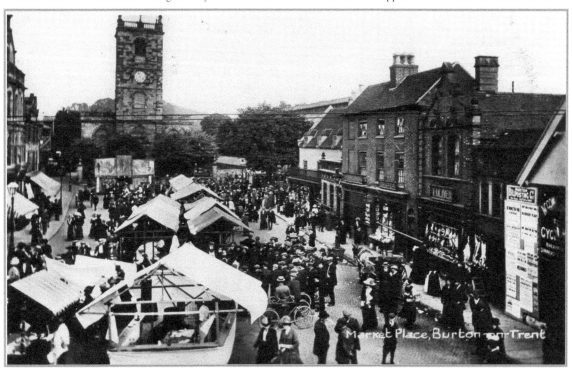

Market Place, Burton-on-Trent

An early market day scene with hardly any of the covered stalls usually associated with markets. The Market Hall opened in 1883 and stands on part of the old abbey grounds. The Man in the Moon public house on the right made way for the Abbey Arcade, which was built in the early 1930s.

In later years the only time the market place was cleared of stalls was when the showman's rides for the annual Statutes Fair were due in the town.

Market Place, Burton-on-Trent

A bustling market day, the like of which many Burton people will fondly remember, probably photographed in the late 1940s or early 1950s. Most of the week's fresh provisions would have been purchased here on a Thursday or Saturday, long before supermarket shopping became the norm.

This unknown local couple entering the Parish Church were surprised to find themselves featured on this postcard by Ernest Abrahams, adding on the back: 'Is it not funny a genuine snapshot taken when we went to Mr Swinterton's wedding on 11th Jan 1910.' It was sent to a Miss Petigrew in Hampshire.

Having crossed the Andressey Bridge, it was a cool stroll through the avenue of trees to the Cherry Orchard.

Looking back towards the Andressey Bridge, a few minutes' walk from the hustle and bustle of the town centre brought people to this quiet spot.

After shopping at the market many families would bring their children to the play area on the right.

Most postcards of the Cherry Orchard only show the keeper's cottage, but this one shows him with his dog and wheelbarrow.

Another scene of the gardens, this one from the 1950s. This was the view that greeted people on entering.

The immaculately laid out gardens and seating with the park keeper's cottage, which was later replaced with an open seated area.

Few people will remember when water ran under the gridded footbridge, from the left into the River Trent behind the Parish Church. This spur dried up many years ago.

An unusual postcard view of the side walk, which was not featured very often.

SEY BRIDGE AND PARISH CHURCH, BURTON-ON-TRENT. (4)

Over the years lots of postcards have featured the Parish Church and the Andressey Bridge, and this one from the 1930s shows them off perfectly.

The Memorial Gardens have always been a quiet retreat for shop and office workers to take a lunch break, and many still do today.

St Margaret's Church stood in Shobnall Street from 1881 until it was demolished in 1970. The entrance to Shobnall Close is now here.

CHURCH OF
S. MARGARET
BURTON

285

A postcard interior view of the magnificent and spacious altar area of St Margaret's.

Christ Church on Uxbridge Street corner. The spire was damaged by the Fauld explosion of 1944 and removed. It has now changed to the Evangelical Church.

Opposite: The Wesleyan Methodist Chapel on Station Street and Union Street corner fell foul of the developers and was demolished in the late 1950s. Just visible on the right is the old library building.

HOLY TRINITY CHURCH
BURTON ON TRENT
FROM THE SOUTH EAST

As this card states, it is looking from the south east at Holy Trinity Church, which stood in Horninglow Street from 1880 until 1973. This was the back of the church.

THE LECTERN
HOLY TRINITY CHURCH
BURTON ON TRENT

The magnificent lectern stood at the front of the church to the right of the pulpit. It was one of the many gifts given to the town by the Bass family.

The original Church of St Chad's in Hunter Street served the parish created in 1903. The present church, erected to the left of this picture, was built between 1905 and 1910.

George Street Chapel is now Holy Trinity. The cottages on the left, which were at the time on Bass Brewery land, have gone. At the time of writing the future of the theatre block on the right is uncertain.

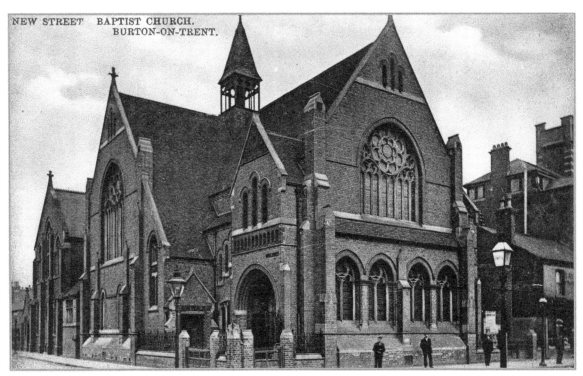

In 1966 a disastrous fire completely destroyed the Baptist Church on New Street–Union Street corner. A National Electrical store now occupies the site.

NEW POST OFFICE, BURTON-ON-TRENT.

A postcard to commemorate the new Post Office. Built by local builders R. Kershaw & Sons, it was opened for business on 9 April 1905. Just visible on the right are the windows of the Crown Inn.

Post office telegraph messenger boys line up outside for a photo shoot. The popularity of sending telegrams is clear from the fact that eight boys are featured, ironically competing with the sending of postcards such as the one on which they are shown.

The GPO indoor staff, numbering 52 people, photographed by Simnetts as a record of the workforce before they moved from their High Street premises to a new location in New Street a year later.

Postal workers on a rare card dating from the time of World War One. With most men away fighting in France the duties of postal delivery were taken up by women and those men too old to enlist.

Interior views of the Post Office are very rare. This one seems to have been taken before the opening in 1905, as the sorting room is in pristine condition and ready for business, with no letters on the sorting frames and no personnel about.

New Street was clearly very quiet in Edwardian days, with the Post Office dominating the street. The public house directly opposite the GPO was the Green Man.

The gardens were always immaculately laid out and well tended, as is clearly shown in this postcard.

The harbour at the top end of the park was always popular with walkers, who would sit and look back over the gardens towards town. The harbour is no longer there.

The Harbour, Outwoods Recreation Grounds, Burton-on-Trent. 1561.

This is a photograph of Outwoods Rec, which has long been enjoyed by courting couples, dog walkers and football players. In its time it has also hosted music concerts, galas and outdoor exhibitions.

Photographed below is the exit out onto Belvoir Road, passing the park keeper's cottage which is just visible behind the trees and bushes.

The area occupied by the bandstand stood at the end of Belvoir Road off Belvedere Road. The A38 bypass now goes through here, having been constructed in the 1960s.

The ornate bandstand was very similar to the one that stood in Stapenhill Gardens, but both are now only distant memories.

Philadelphia Stores on the Station Street–High Street corner shortly before being demolished in 1901. It was replaced by the Grand Clothing Hall, itself eventually making way for a branch of Barclays Bank.

The imposing White Hart Hotel in High Street almost directly opposite the marketplace, remembered by many Burtonians to this day. For many years the hiring of servants and farmhands took place in this building at the time of the Statutes Fair.

"WHITE HART" FAMILY & COMMERCIAL HOTEL,
BURTON-ON-TRENT.
JOHN OULTON, PROPRIETOR.

Whitehurst, Stationer, Burton.

A very old postcard view of the White Horse Inn, which disappeared in the early part of the last century. The Market Hotel then stood on this site for well over 50 years before also closing. A solicitors' practice now occupies this site – 158 High Street.

While this is primarily a view of the old Town Hall, it does also clearly show two of Burton's old, vanished public houses. Visible on the left is the Man in the Moon, while on the right can be seen the sign belonging to the Elephant and Castle.

The Station public house, now converted into apartments, photographed around 1904. This was a popular place for people who had just arrived by train or those whiling away time before making a rail journey.

This promotional postcard was issued shortly after the Wyggeston Hotel had opened in the early 1900s. E.J. Hall was one of the first licencees.

The Staffordshire Knot opposite the County Court in Station Street awaiting redevelopment. The man is looking in the window of the shop that used to be Coltman & Co., ironmongers, who also supplied firearms and ammunition. By the time this photograph was taken the large wooden double-barrelled shotgun that used to hang above the shop doorway had disappeared, its fate unknown.

Level crossing gates and the Mayors Arm's public house standing where the roadway to Worthington Way is now. The Mayor's Arms lost its licence together with the New Inn, which stood on the opposite side of Station Street, to make way for a new public house. This was the Locomotive, so named to celebrate the crossing in this photograph.

This photograph shows numbers 160–161 Horninglow Street, the property that at one time was the Rising Sun public house. Burton's new police station now occupies this site.

The Waggoners Inn with George Angel's shop and cottages in Horninglow Street, all of which were demolished in 1987. The ground was taken over by Ind Coope Brewery before later passing to Bass and then finally to Coors. This area is now covered with trees and bushes.

The Bell Hotel, photographed here in the early 1900s, was originally part of Samuel Allsop's Brewery in Horninglow Street. Outside is an early local charabanc and its passengers posing for the photograph.

After closing as a hotel, the Bell had many varied uses over the years. For many years it was the headquarters of the North Staffordshire TA and also the Air Training Corps, but it has since been converted into apartments. The public house on the left is the Bell Inn.

The victorious Ind Coope Burton Breweries Cup-winning team from 1937 are featured on this postcard. The team was R.A. Jones, C.H. Jones, J. Burdett, A. Payton, E. Dickinson, A. Ordish (wicketkeeper), F. Garner, K. Woolley, G. Robinson, J. Ellis, F. Gould (captain). They declared their innings at 398 for 8 and so the last two named did not bat.

The losing finalists in that match were Marstons. They were represented by H. Bridges, L. Bunting, A. Brown, J. Cresswell, S.J.A. Evershead, L. Marshment, J. Green (captain), E. Bladen, C. Smith, F. Caulton, J. Powell (wicketkeeper). In a high-scoring game they only lost by 12 runs, being all out for 386.

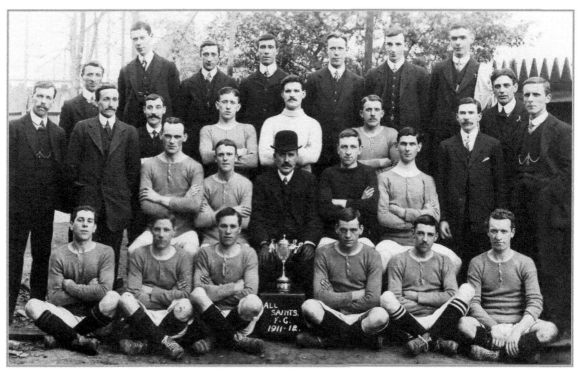

Postcards of winners of the Burton & District Challenge Cup were not often published, but it was decided to make the 1911–12 Final, to be played on 9 May 1912, a representative match to raise funds for the tragic *Titanic* disaster that had occurred only a month earlier. All Saints had only three of their own players in the side, the rest of which was made up of local players and league guests. Opponents Shobnall Villa had only one of their players – Wright – in their team, and the other 10 came from Chelsea, Manchester City, Aston Villa and Barnsley, among others. All Saints won 1–0 and £35 was raised.

It seems Push-Ball was a very popular spectator sport at this time, judging from the size of the crowd. Details of this game are unknown but the location is definitely Peel Croft, which when this card was produced was the home of Burton United and previously Burton Swifts. It is believed this is the only surviving view of the ground from when Burton had a team playing League football in English League Division Two.

PUSH-BALL
FORRESTERS · V · NEWHALL.

Crown green bowls has always been popular in Burton and the surrounding district. On this postcard three boys are enjoying a game at Shobnall Fields, and the original café and changing room block can be seen in the background.

Early 1900s aviation meetings were always popular with Burtonians, who would turn out in their hundreds to watch this new 'sport' of flying. Many postcards of these meetings still exist.

M. Salmet at Burton.

Upon winning the prestigious Berry Cup at Nottingham Regatta, Trent Rowing Club issued a special postcard to recognise their success.

Burton Leander Rowing Club have enjoyed many achievements over the years. The crew and cox sit proudly with their City of Bath and Trent Challenge trophies, two of the 12 trophies the rowing club won in 1911.

Ardath Tobacco Co. Ltd produced several series of local football teams around the country. In 1936 Burton and District were featured in the Midland League set, and Public Services FC where number 82.

PUBLIC SERVICES (BURTON-ON-TRENT) F.C.

There were eight top-quality photocards to collect, issued with cigarettes. The others featured were Winshill Amateurs number 80, Grange Swifts number 81, Burton Town number 83, Burton YMCA number 84, Mount Pleasant number 85, Newton Solney number 86 and Newhall Colts number 87.

WINSHILL AMATEURS F.C.

Members of Burton Football Club second team posing before the start of the 1905–06 season. By this time the club had already been in existence for over 30 years.

The Leander Hockey Club were one of several teams in Burton in Edwardian times. While not one of the leading hockey clubs, they were still able to field two teams.

Burton Town FC were only in existence from the 1924–25 season until the outbreak of World War Two in the 1939–40 season. Here their reserves and officials pose with the Bass Charity Vase and the Burton & District Challenge Cup, both won in 1931–32.

The opening of the greens for the new bowls season each year was always eagerly awaited. Here, Mr Harold Elks, watched by members, rolls up the first wood of an early 1960s season on the Scalpcliffe House Green, the Stapenhill branch of Burton Working Men's Club on Stapenhill Road.

Works sports days were always a favourite fun day out for the workforce and their families. Here, competitors line up before one of the novelty races at Ind Coope's Belvedere Road ground in the late 1940s.

All of the competitions at works sports days kept the crowd entertained. The event photographed below was at the same sports day as above, and was event 14 (as indicatd by the board), the tug of war. There is no indication which department this team represented.

King Edward Place was named after the visit of Edward VII in 1902, when he commented that the view of the magnificent St Paul's was hampered by the properties of St Paul's Street East, which stood to the left of this scene. They were subsequently demolished to leave the open view that is there today.

The Town Hall was always popular for postcard views, and this and the previous card can be dated to before and after 1910, this being the year Lord Burton's statue was erected.

The borough's gas department pulled out all the stops for George V's coronation in 1911. With gas lighting still in its infancy, the decoration on the Town Hall was magnificent, especially the caricatures of the king and queen.

As well as the use of new gas lighting, night-time photography was also being experimented with. Local photographer J.S. Simmett soon acquired these skills.

This is a lovely shot of Michael Arthur Bass first Baron Burton's statue, together with one of his family's many gifts to the town, that of St Paul's Church. It was hoped that should Burton one day be granted city status then St Paul's would be the city's cathedral.

In this 1960s postcard of King Edward Place, the viewing platform under the clock can be seen above the canopied entrance. This was added for the visit of Queen Elizabeth II in 1957 for her to salute the crowds.

These two rare postcards show the extension to the Town Hall being carried out by local building contractors Thomas Lowe of Curzan Street on the site formally occupied by Butts Mantle Warehouse.

The extension was finally completed in September 1938, and a plaque to commemorate this is affixed to the angled frontage at the right of the picture.

Local trade exhibitions have been held at the Town Hall for many years. This one, which showed the advantages of electricity, was the Winter Fair of 1934.

Geo. Henson's of Parker Street presented this magnificent display of their varied bottling techniques at another trade show. When this postcard was produced they were one of the leading bottling companies in Burton.

THE BURTON BREWERY COMPANY, BURTON-ON-TRENT.

The Burton Brewery Company premises stood at the Bargates End of High Street from 1842–1914 before becoming part of Worthingtons. This is the back of the building looking from The Hay.

Although the caption on this postcard reads Ind Coope, it is in fact a view of Bass & Ind Coope, the brick wall running across the middle, with the cart beside it, being the boundary.

MESSRS IND COOPE & C$\underline{os}$ BREWERY BURTON.

Interior shots of brewery premises were sometimes issued. This one of the mashroom shows it in pristine condition, having obviously been spruced up for the picture.

In this photograph of the Bass internal railway system, the locomotive is pulling the director's carriage. The large building in the background became the Bass Museum and later Coors Visitors' Centre. Houses in Brook Street are visible in the distance.

The middle yard workforce pose for this postcard view in the early 1900s. The roadway is looking from High Street towards Guild Street.

Looking from the Hay Wharf, this was the Bass Old Brewery in High Street. The water tower is all that is left of these buildings.

None of the buildings or chimneys seen on this postcard have survived, having all been cleared in the modernisation and reorganisation of the brewery over the years.

This is a picture of Allsopp's Cooperage in Station Street, where almost all of the cleaning and repairing of returned casks was done outside before dispatching them around the brewery by rail.

Samuel Allsopp's large brewery building with, in the foreground, the taxi hansom cabs outside their restroom, prior to being summoned to the station to pick up passengers.

A very large workforce making their way down the brewery yard, all eager to take a well-earned break.

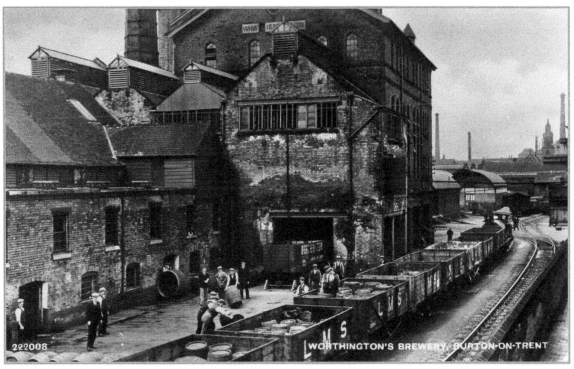

Worthington Brewery looking from High Street to Station Street. The rail line is now the route of Worthington Way, and the buildings were replaced by Burton Place.

The Derby Street site of Trueman's Brewery. The proximity to the main rail lines from the brewery sidings made for speedy delivery of their ales. On production of this card the printers put Burton Brewery, but it should read Buxton Brewery.

An early print was used on this postcard to promote Burton Red Label, published by local printers W.B. Darley.

Ind Coope & Allsopp's shunting crew are quite happy to take a few minutes to pose for the photographer in the late 1950s.

Ind Coope's early bottling stores were very cluttered with hardly any of the bottling operation done mechanically. Over 30 men can be seen here, although this would not be the total workforce. The gentleman in the front right seems to be the bottling manager, and the two men to his right in the white jackets are probably foremen.

The coopers take a few minutes' break from making and repairing various wooden firkins, kilderkins and barrels to have their photograph taken.

A delightful aerial shot used on a postcard by brewery reps to promote Marstons on Shobnall Road.

Almost all the buildings through the gates are now gone, but the horse-mounting block at the foot of the steps belonging to Mr Bass is still there today. The gateway also survives but is now wider.

132 S.   HIGH ST. ENTRANCE BASS'S BREWERY, BURTON-ON-TRENT.

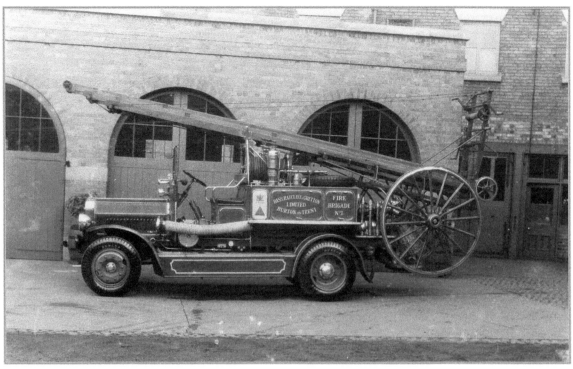

Here is one of the Bass fire engines outside the brewery fire station off Guild Street, which was built adjacent to the old shire horse stables. The door to the right led to the fire superintendent's office.

Ind Coope's fire service on parade outside the internal fire station with the large ex-army ambulance, probably in the late 1950s. The large building is the back of Ind Coope's B Block offices.

Looking into the middle yard brewery from Guild Street towards High Street, with a brewery floater disappearing into the distance. Nothing in this scene has survived.

Unbelievably high mountains of casks inside Bass. Pyramids like these were common in most breweries in the town, so having to stack them high was something the men were used to.

A dramatic photograph of the 1954 fire in Ind Coope's hop stores. The brewery brigade seem to have the situation under control, while a large crowd watched the event from the safe distance of Station Street.

The steaming shed of Ind Coope where returned dirty casks were washed and steam cleaned ready for use. Some of the men pictured would probably be 'sniffers', who did the final check for cleanliness by smelling inside each cask.

A postcard of the tub inside which the king started the mash process of 400 barrels of King's Ale on his visit to Bass on Saturday 22 February 1902.

Local photographers Simnetts used still life poses to celebrate the occasion. Here the photographer has put a bottle of King's Ale alongside a picture of the king and has nipped along from his Guild Street studio to the Guild Tavern, on the same street, for one of their bottled beers to complete the picture.

Mr Cornelius O'Sullivan FRS FIC was chief chemist of Bass and one of Europe's leading brewery chemists. He oversaw the King's Ale production run.

A perfectly posed shot of the workforce who had had the task of capping, labelling and crating the finished bottles.

This card was sent from a son to his father asking if he was still alive! Perhaps the man drinking reminded him of his father who might have liked a tipple.

Riding his "Hobby Horse" at
222 **BURTON-on-TRENT.**

A card published in France that Jacksons of Burton overprinted to extol the virtues of Bass No. 1 bottled beer.

DROP OF GOOD "OLD BURTON"
Bass's No. 1.

"I'll warrant it proved
an excuse for the
glass."

His only pair
at
Burton-on-Trent

What the significance was of this postcard, posted in 1906, asking about a pair of trousers, we shall never know.

A postcard issued to be used all over Europe in the early 1900s. Someone obviously thought it apt to ask if these were the goings on in Burton.

DO WE DO THESE THINGS AT BURTON.

This card from 1912 was sent from Stapenhill to Birmingham and features an interesting play on words!

Someone staying at the now disappeared Tiger Inn at Hawkins Lane sent this to a Mr Frank Wilson of Leicester. What Frank made of the suggestion is a mystery.

This postcard, obviously intended for a seaside resort, somehow came to be used in Burton over 100 miles from the coast.

At first glance it would seem this card was heralding the end of the tramway system in Burton, but as it was posted in 1911, almost 20 years before the last tram ran, it is clear it was meant to represent the last tram home in an evening.

Michael Arthur Bass, regarded as one of the outstanding Burtonians of all time, was born in High Street in 1837 and made Lord Burton in 1886. He was photographed here in 1903, six years before he died.

Harriet Georgina Thornewill of the Burton Engineering family married Michael Arthur Bass in 1869 in Stretton Church. She was always ready to give her support to local fundraising and social functions.

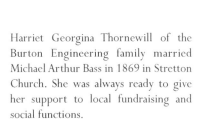

Local photographer Ernest Abrahams took this photograph of a member of the local constabulary in the early 1900s. The man's name is unknown.

All we know of this lady is that her name was Muriel and she was a conductress on the Midland Red buses.

The Strollers could be booked for singing concerts by contacting local agent Mr J. Langley of Woodville. These photographs were also sold 'for the benefit of the *Burton Daily Mail* Uncle Jack Convalescent Fund for Poor Children'.

The Burton Pierrots were available for fêtes, carnival processions and garden parties. This postcard shows them in 1905.

Photographed before starting their displays at the Burton Aviation meeting in 1910 are early flying pioneers Bruneau de Laborie, who crashed his plane on landing, and Paul de Lesseps, son of the man behind the building of the Suez Canal.

A rare photograph of the Burton Rifle Volunteers under rifle instruction before leaving for South Africa in 1899. The location was probably Burton Meadows.

This stern-looking gentleman had his photograph taken by Simnetts, probably to commemorate him working as commissionaire at Truman, Hanbury & Buxtons Brewery in Derby Street.

MAJOR RATCLIFF M.P
1706 BURTON DIVISION OF STAFFORDSHIRE COPYRIGHT

Major Robert Frederick Ratcliff, adopted as Unionist Party MP for Burton in 1900, returned in 1906, 1910 and 1911 but gave way to John Gretton in 1918. He also commanded the 1/6th North Staffordshire Regiments in World War One and was first out of the trenches on 12 October 1915 when 70 per cent of his men were wounded.

As this postcard states, this is the Bass trip of 1911 arriving at Blackpool. In all, the popular excursions for Bass employees to Blackpool took place eight times, this being the last. The men, women and children, all in their Sunday best, getting off train number 15, were possibly from the blacksmiths, excavators and wheelwrights departments.

On a beautiful summer's day in July 1914 these members of Carlton Street United Methodist Sunday School pose on their annual treat, a trip, it is believed, to Barton-under-Needwood. It seems the Sunday School was well patronised as there are quite a number of children present.

This postcard was produced in 1918. Dr Holford (in the trilby) kept his own practice and attended patients at the General Hospital as well as overseeing the Red Cross Hospital at the Town Hall. Dr Thompson, Commandant Miss Mary Thompson (centre, awarded the OBE in 1918), her quartermaster on her right and Sister Valley are also in the photograph.

Pictured at the same time in October, a month before the hostilities ended, are Sister Cooke, Mrs Gerrard, Nurse Edwards, Sister Shortland and Mrs Heath. They all served the Town Hall wards.

Over the years J.S. Simnetts Photographers would pop next door to the Opera House in Guild Street to record the artists in the various productions, many postcards of which survive. Miss Winifred Goodhead has signed this card, photographed during her appearance as Little Violett, one of the geisha girls in the opera *Geisha,* in 1924.

Pictured together in 1979, shortly before their disbandment, are Ind Coope's internal fire crew. From left to right are Tony Harrison, Jack Roberts, Dave Barrett, Roy Marsland, Brian Chinn, George Holland, Mike Skinner (fire chief), Dave Jones, Bob Smith, Mick Cotton, Pete Mathews, Ken Hextall and Terry Myatt.

The coronation of Queen Elizabeth II in 1953 was celebrated all over the country, with Burton being no exception. There were shop displays, processions, concerts, house decoration and fancy dress competitions. In this photograph the children of the Bass fire brigade and their families have lined up to show their costumes. On the front row, left to right, are John Mills, Terry Garner, Veronica Mills, Miss Goodhead, Barbara Jeffries, Shirley Jeffries, Linda Bache, Paul Bache and Terry Brassington.

On 22 June 1911 a service to celebrate the coronation of King George V took place at Burton Parish Church after a procession from the Town Hall. Shown on this postcard are part of the line up passing the County Court. The coronation choir are leading, followed by representatives from the church, law and medical profession.

At the start of World War One in 1914 many local men made a visit to Simnetts to get a photograph to leave with loved ones. This one is of Private 2836 Arthur H. Garner of the 1/6th North Staffordshire Regiment.

Photographed here is the visit of the Prince of Wales, later King Edward VIII, on 21 July 1929. Here he can be seen talking to William Coltman VC at the war memorial. Members of the British Legion line the steps and Private Garner has returned safely and can be seen standing to the left of the standard bearer.

A Burton Brewery Company horse and cart, probably on their way back to High Street after making a rural delivery.

Brewery floaters, although used extensively by the breweries, were not very often photographed. This winter scene passing the then Midland Hotel shows one beautifully. The dray man is obviously quite happy to let the horse make its own way back to the brewery while he attempts to keep warm.

Bass replaced their steam locomotives with diesel engines towards the end of the brewery railway system's usage. This one is crossing Station Street just before George Street. At that time, Currys had a small store at 178 Station Street.

A. Machin & Sons local garage supplied this delivery van to Roberts & Birch Butchers of Mosely Street in the late 1940s.

All over advertising was popular decoration for Corporation buses at one time, as can be seen on this one passing Johnson's the florist on High Street in 1970. It is probably suggesting that if Ind Coope's Burton Ale had been sampled it was safer to take the bus home!

A busy market day in 1962 as the number 5 bus picks up passengers outside the Abbey Arcade congestion was often caused by cars being able to park in the street.

Photographed at the Sentinel works at Shrewsbury, a Sentinel-Garner with trade plates is about to leave for delivery to J.B. Kinds Ltd. The legal speed for this tractor and trailer was 20mph and road tax was £50.

Another new Sentinel for J.B. Kinds, this time carrying an extra trailer. J.B. Kinds Ltd ceased trading from their Shobnall Street site in 2008.

One of the Bass 0–4–0 saddle tank locomotives, which were a familiar sight criss-crossing the town moving the brewery stock over the many level crossings until the end of the 1960s.

This is a very rare postcard view of a derailment. As can be seen, three policemen and a large crowd of onlookers were at the scene by the time the photographer had arrived.

A decorated double decker in the depot yard, photographed before setting off as the last open-platform, crew-operated bus in Burton. Leaving at 6.31pm on Saturday 3 January 1981 from Wetmore Park to Edge Hill, it arrived back at the depot at 10.45pm after extensively covering the town.

Passing Stockbridge's drapers, at the time of this photograph one of Burton's oldest established firms, the number 1 bus makes its way up Station Street en route to Stapenhill. This area is now pedestrianised.

Burton Breweries always supported local charities, as is shown on the van in the photograph. Ind Coope and Bass combined funds to provide this for the WVS in Guild Street in 1961.

This busy scene at the foot of the Station Bridge is quite unique as all the vehicles carry the Burton registration of FA. Registrations for Burton began with FA in 1903, ending with UFA in 1964.

An Everard's steam articulated wagon, which would make frequent trips from the Leicester Brewery to Everard's in Anglesey Road.

Two Ind Coope delivery vehicles outside what were the bottling stores on Shobnall Road (now IMEX Business Park), showing the old yellow and black livery and the new white and bottle green. This photograph was taken in 1958.

Corporation car number 22 poses on the Horninglow–Branston road route before setting off.

As three B&A Light Railway cars are about to move off, taking a Sunday school on an outing, it seems everyone wanted to be in the photograph. Burton Corporation trams can always be told apart from B&A cars as their destination boards were at the front of the top deck, while B&A boards were situated above the head of the driver.

Local breweries all had steam lorries at some time. With its solid wheels and open cab, here one of Allsopp's is shown in the garage.

Photographed before being delivered to Allsopp's, their new long-based, open-cabbed lorry is outside the body-works in Surrey.

A photograph of number 16 of the Burton Corporation bus fleet on the number 1 bus route, negotiating the then narrow junction at Bargates from Bridge Street into High Street.

A short-lived transport scheme that was tried in the town was the Burton Buxi, a bus that could be hailed to stop like a taxi. It ran from the Town Hall to New Street bus park and back again for a modest 5p fare either way.

Double Diamond certainly worked wonders for this Ind Coope float as it took third prize in the Lichfield Bower procession at Whitsun in 1958.

A British Rail Austin and Scammell 'Hobby Horse' making a delivery of casks of Cream Sherry for bottling at Grants of St James's in Station Street. The large office block behind has now been converted into apartments and there is a housing complex on the yard area.

May & Armstrong House Furnishers were situated at number 26 Station Street, Burton. Here, a delivery driver poses with his van at Cadley Hill, Swadlincote, in 1949.

The 'Bass Bottle' was created in the late 1950s for use by the advertising department of Bass. It carried all manner of advertising for use in pubs, clubs and any other outlets for Bass products.

Ladounge flying over Burton.
Burton Aviation Meeting 1910.

The Aviation Meeting took place on Bass Meadow and this photograph is a view towards the gasometers on Wetmore Road. This new form of transport was viewed by many hundreds of Burtonians at the various meetings.

An alternative view of the Aviation Meeting to the previous one, this time with Newton Road and Winshill in the background. The accident mentioned occurred on landing and the plane sustained quite a lot of damage, but, fortunately, the pilot Laborie escaped unhurt.

LABORIE FLYING AT BURTON BEFORE THE ACCIDENT.

An early picture of the disastrous flood of 1875, showing the junction with Guild Street and, in the distance, the original Holy Trinity Church with its square bell tower. The houses on the left, past the Plough Inn, were later demolished to make way for the Burton Magistrates' Court.

Another card showing the flood, but this one was issued some years after the event. It seems everyonre wanted to be in the photograph regardless of any health hazard. Christ Church is just visible in the distance.

NEW STREET, BURTON-ON-TRENT, DURING FLOOD OF 1875

FLOODS

Floods like these were a frequent happening after heavy rains until well into the 1960s when extensive dredging of the River Trent took place. This view is looking along Guild Street towards the police station, with Guild Tavern on the left.

This time looking in the opposite direction, the floods did not stop the Bass internal railway system. The signalman was probably wondering what was going on.

Horninglow Street with the junction with Hawkins Lane just out of shot on the left. These cyclists were obviously not going to let a simple thing like flooding stop them from going to work.

This photograph is a good picture to show how much the Trent used to flood. Its level is just visible through the arch of the Trent Bridge. Taken from outside the old baths, Nunnerley's old brewery building can be seen on the left.

The gardens and flower beds will be remembered by many local people. A treat for the children in those days was going for a walk to see the goldfish in the pool in the forefront of the picture, with the ornamental swan also surrounded by water before it was deemed a danger to small children.

This, the first viewcard to feature the new second river crossing, St Peter's Bridge, was issued in 1986. The bridge had been officially opened by Linda Chalker MP, then the Minister of State for Transport, on 14 November 1985.

The Rockery,Stapenhill Gardens.(1)

The rock gardens viewed from Stapenhill Road with many brewery chimneys dominating the skyline. The gulley way was the ancient course of the water from the hills down into the River Trent.

Looking back towards the entrance from Stapenhill Road, the large house is number 14 Stapenhill Road. These gardens were always well maintained, with pathways either side of the gulley for people to stroll along and enjoy the flowers. This area is hardly recognisable from the two pictures today.

ROCK GARDENS, STAPENHILL, BURTON-ON-TRENT.

K.5480.

Walking off Main Street on to where Stapenhill House once stood would lead to the Fairy Dell, shown here when still beautifully maintained by the Corporation Gardens Department.

Dr Clay's house once stood where these ornate gardens are, situated next to Stapenhill Church. Many wedding photographs have been taken here over the years.

The Stone Arbour, Burton Recreation Grounds.

Many people who had just walked through the grounds would rest on the seats in the arbour before exiting on to Stapenhill Road at the Trent Bridge End. The arbour, which resembles a castle, has not survived very well.

The stone grotto in the foreground was built with stone blocks from the original Burton Bridge. In this view the banks of the Trent were very close to the grotto, whereas these days the banks have been moved further out.

STAPENHILL RECREATION
GROUND, BURTON-ON-TRENT

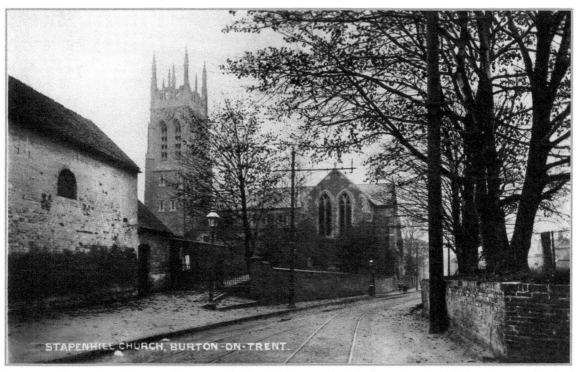

An autumnal scene from the time of the trams. The large building on the left adjoined number 90 Main Street, and both of these were demolished in the 1930s.

This card was issued after the new grounds had been laid out on the site of the large private properties that once stood here. The brick archway is what was left of the garden walls of Dr Clay's house.

LOVER'S WALK. BURTON ON TRENT.

Although this card says simply 'Lover's Walk', it will be recognised by many as being part of Stapenhill Gardens.

These lads pose for the photographer beside the ornate bandstand in the gardens. The main entrance to the seating around the bandstand was through the gateway directly opposite the cemetery gates. It was removed in the early 1960s.

It is very doubtful you would see this scene as quiet nowadays as it is in this view. It was probably issued to show the improved junction. The old tram lines are just visible.

Stapenhill Memorial at the St Peter's Street and Main Street junction. At every Memorial Sunday in November wreaths are laid here to remember the Stapenhill men who fell in the world wars.

Although this postcard shows Stapenhill Church, it also features the precarious footbridge across to the Oxhay. The man sitting on it is probably enjoying a lovely summer's day.

44/2 Anglesey Bridge, Burton-on-Trent

The printers of this card, not knowing the area, got their titles mixed up. This is clearly the Ferry Bridge looking towards the Stapenhill viaduct across to town.

The Ferry Bridge.   Burton-on-Trent.
26.1.03.
This Bridge built by Lord Burton, was a great boon to the public, as they no longer have to cross the river in a little boa as they used to years ago. Love to all from Norah.

Although it had been 14 years since the above bridge had opened in 1889, Norah thought it still significant to mention it on the postcard she was sending.

The ferryman posing on his boat before the Ferry Bridge replaced him. People wanting to be ferried across the river from the town side stood where the two men are on the pier and would call 'Ferry' to the cottage on the far bank, hoping the weather was not too bad for the ferryman to turn out.

THE OLD FERRY.   BURTON ON TRENT.

This view is looking back towards the bottom of Stanton Road, and the buildings on the right-hand side of the road are ready for demolition to create pedestrian access to the Holly Green housing project.

Seven houses, numbers 19–25 St Peter's Street, along with three empty shops that had previously been a radio and television repair shop, a chemist and a general shop, were all removed in the early 1980s to remove the severe corner that led to the run on to St Peter's Bridge, which would be accessed where the trees are in the distance.

Playing Fields & Rockery, Stapenhill.

This elevated view has clearly been taken from the top of Stapenhill Church. The playing fields on Stapenhill Hollow were used for many years by various Stapenhill cricket teams for their home games. The Whit Monday sports also took place here before being cancelled.

A quiet stroll along this pathway was a favourite with many Burtonians, particularly on a Sunday afternoon before making their way towards the Ferry Bridge and back into town.

STAPENHILL GARDENS,
BURTON ON TRENT

The buildings on Main Street, from where the hand cart is on the left-hand side into the distance, have long since disappeared. The Corporation tram just passing Stapenhill Institute, is heading for the terminus at the top of Ferry Street and the men to the left of the tram are outside the old Punch Bowl Inn.

Standing a little further back than the previous photograph, this view shows the Barley Mow (now the Barley) on the right. The large beech tree in the front garden of number 72 dominated that side of the road for over 200 years before having to be removed after contracting a killer disease which meant it could fall onto the traffic.

St Mark's Church was the terminus for the Corporation trams. The last car to leave this route did so on 31 December 1929, the end of the tram system in Burton.

Car number 19 careered back down Bearwood Hill Road on 8 October 1919 while en route to Ashby. There were two fatalities, a female passenger and the conductress, Miss Lilian Parker, who died later from her injuries.

Winshill.

A card showing old Winshill with St Mark's Church dominating the skyline. It was probably intended for local use as it only carries the caption Winshill.

A postcard of the Ada Chadwick School when it was still a secondary modern. In July 1975, together with the High School and Boys' Grammar School, it formed the Abbot Beyne School.

Ada Chadwick School, Winshill

Two cards issued to show the new Manners Estate shops built in the 1950s to serve the council houses.

The shopping centre, while still there, has changed considerably since this postcard was issued.

A series of postcard views were commissioned to show off the new council estate.

Another view of Melbourne Avenue. Almost all of these properties would have been occupied when the photograph was taken, but only one woman and her pram seem to be about.

Brough Road, Old Winshill.

Brough Road when it still resembled a very rural scene with a few cottages, no proper roads laid out and no street lighting.

Almost all the properties in this view, from the houses on the left to the school buildings on the right, with the exception of the church and the house pictured in front of it, have been removed following the redevelopment of this part of Winshill.

Hawfield Lane, Winshill.

A Corporation tram on its way to the terminus outside Winshill Church, travelling along Bearwood Hill Road. The delivery boy on the right is more interested in the photographer than in the passing tram.

Moving forward approximately 40 years, this is another postcard view taken from almost exactly the same spot. Apart from the disappearance of the trams and the erection of street lighting, nothing seems to have changed.

Bearwood Hill Road, Winshill

BEARWOOD HILL ROAD, BURTON-ON-TRENT.

J. C. PERFECT & Co.

The first Winshill tram of Burton Corporation Tramways can be seen here negotiating Bearwood Hill in 1903. It was - carrying local dignitaries and had been decorated with flags and bunting for the occasion.

A Corporation tram beginning the climb up Bearwood Hill on a local viewcard, upon which someone has printed a verse for use as a Christmas card.

The townsman, 'neath King Christmas' jovial rule
Rejoicing, wends his (no more "weary") way,
As in our Burton trams he travels, gay,
Merry of heart, to keep the festive Yule.

Nina Serêtte.

A Burton and Ashby Light Railway car entering Ashby Road from High Bank Road. It was rumoured trams took this route through Winshill because residents on Ashby Road did not want this form of noisy transport passing their properties.

Burton's beacon in the countrywide line for King George V's coronation was situated on Waterloo Mount, photographed here with the top of the water tower visible behind the trees.

There is not a car to be seen either parked or travelling along here in this quiet scene, a complete contrast to nowadays.

In this 1950s view of Church Hill Street the overhead tram cable stanchions can be seen, still intact after 30 years.

One of Burton's most devastating fires took place at Peach's Maltings in Wood Street on 12 July 1908. Postcards were produced showing the destruction.

Owner Robert Peach stayed at the scene all night helping firemen fight the blaze. It was estimated that at least £10,000 worth of top malt was destroyed.

Attended by Bass and Allsopp's fire brigades as well as the Corporation fire service, the fire lasted four days. It wasn't until 3 o'clock in the morning that they started to get it under control.

The steam produced from fighting the fire could be seen for miles. It was reported it could be seen as far away as Rugeley, 21 miles away. Thousands came from surrounding villages to witness the tragic event.

Iron girders buckled because of the heat and walls bulged under the pressure of the malt swelling.

Workers spent days clearing and sorting the grain. After rebuilding the maltings they were used as a billet for the 1/6th Staffordshire Regiment before they left for France.

A view from the 1900s.

A view from the 1920s.

A view from the 1930s.

A view from the 1940s.

A view from the 1950s.

A view from the 1960s.

A view from the 1970s.

A view from the 1980s.

ND - #0371 - 270225 - C0 - 260/195/10 - PB - 9781780914213 - Gloss Lamination